MW00783788

BLESS YORE BEAUTIFUL HIDE

Words by JOHNNY MERCER
Music by GENE de PAUL

3

WHEN YOU'RE IN LOVE

Words by JOHNNY MERCER
Music by GENE de PAUL

When You're In Love

JUNE BRIDE

Words by JOHNNY MERCER
Music by GENE de PAUL

Moderately with expression

Oh, they say when you mar-ry in June __ you're a bride __ all your life; __ And the bride-groom who mar-ries in June __ gets a

9

LONESOME POLECAT

Words by JOHNNY MERCER
Music by GENE de PAUL

SPRING, SPRING, SPRING!

Words by JOHNNY MERCER
Music by GENE de PAUL

SOBBIN' WOMEN

Words by JOHNNY MERCER
Music by GENE de PAUL

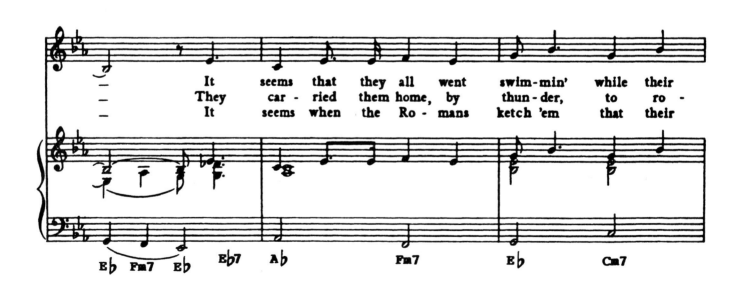

Sobbin' Women

REFRAIN

Them a wo-men was sob-bin', sob-bin', sob-bin' fit_ to be tied_____
Them a wo-men was sob-bin', sob-bin', sob-bin' pass-in' the nights_____
Them a wo-men was sob-bin', sob-bin', sob-bin' buck-ets o' tears_____
(E-ven though they're all) sob-bin', sob-bin', sob-bin' weep-in' a ton_____

Eb   Fm7   Eb   Ab   Eb   Fm7

_ Ev-'ry mus-cle was throb-bin', throb-bin' from that ri - o-tous ride._____ Seems they
_While the Ro-mans was go-in' out hob nob-bin' start-in' up fights._____ They kept
_ On ac-count o' old dob-bin, dob-bin, real-ly rat-tled their ears._____ Oh, they
_ Just re-mem-ber what Rob-in, Rob-in Rob-in Hood would-a done._____ We'll be

Eb   Eb   Fm7   Eb   Cm7   Fm   Fm7   Bb7

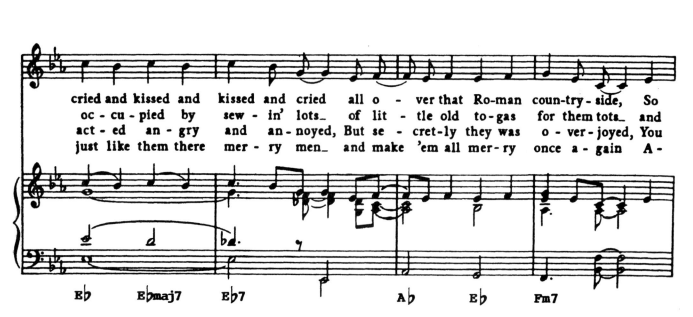

cried and kissed and kissed and cried all o - ver that Ro-man coun-try-side, So
oc-cu-pied by sew-in' lots_ of lit-tle old to-gas for them tots_ and
act-ed an-gry and an-noyed, But se-cret-ly they was o-ver-joyed, You
just like them there mer-ry men_ and make 'em all mer-ry once a-gain A-

Eb   Ebmaj7   Eb7   Ab   Eb   Fm7

Sobbin' Women

Sobbin' Women

GOIN' CO'TIN'

Words by JOHNNY MERCER
Music by GENE de PAUL

23

WONDERFUL, WONDERFUL DAY

Words by JOHNNY MERCER
Music by GENE de PAUL

26

Wonderful, wonderful day

Wonderful, wonderful day